6

Prentice Hall
Math

Skill Builder

Unit 3: Ratio, Proportion, and Percent

PEARSON

Prentice
Hall

Boston, Massachusetts

Upper Saddle River, New Jersey

Pearson Prentice Hall™ is a trademark of Pearson Education, Inc.
Pearson® is a registered trademark of Pearson plc.
Prentice Hall® is a registered trademark of Pearson Education, Inc.

ISBN 0-13-201504-8

3 4 5 6 7 8 9 10   09   08   07   06

TABLE OF CONTENTS

UNIT 3: Ratio, Proportion, and Percent

NAME _____ DATE _____

RATIOS

A **ratio** is a comparison of two quantities.

The ratio of footballs to basketballs shown at the right is $\frac{3}{2}$. This ratio can also be written as 3:2 and 3 to 2.

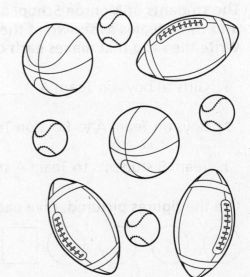

Example

Give the ratio comparing the number of baseballs to the total number of balls shown.

Four out of nine balls shown are baseballs. The ratio of baseballs to balls shown can be written as 4 to 9, 4:9, or $\frac{4}{9}$.

GUIDED PRACTICE

Use the letters in the box.

| A C C C L |
| L L L L O |
| O O R R R |
| R R |

1. How many letters are there in all? _____

2. How many letters are Rs? _____

3. How many letters are Os? _____

4. Give the ratio of Rs to Os. _____

5. Give the ratio of Os to Rs. _____

6. Give the ratio of Rs to all letters in three ways. _____

In a group of students, 35 are right-handed and 6 are left-handed.

7. Give the ratio of right-handers to left-handers. _____

8. Give the ratio of left-handers to right-handers. _____

9. Give the ratio of right-handers to all students. _____

10. Give the ratio of left-handers to all students. _____

NOW YOU TRY IT!

The students at Monroe School are divided into three teams as shown at the right. Write the ratio that makes each comparison.

	Team A	Team B	Team C
Girls	50	72	65
Boys	57	49	58

1. Girls to boys on Team A _____

2. Boys on Team A to Boys on Team C _____

3. Team B students to Team A students _____

Use the figures pictured. Give each ratio.

○ ○ ○ ○ □ □ □ □ □ ◺ ◺

4. Squares to circles _____   5. Triangles to squares _____

6. Circles to triangles _____   7. Triangles to all figures _____

8. Write the ratio of circles to squares in three ways. _____

Problem Solving

Last season, the Yorktown football team won 6 games, lost 3 games and tied 1 game. Tell what each ratio compares.

9. 6 to 3 _____

10. 3 to 10 _____

11. 7 to 3 _____

12. A recipee calls for 3 cups of olive oil and 2 cups of balsamic vinegar. What is the ratio of olive oil to balsamic vinegar? _____

TEST PREP

13. Give the ratio of Os to Xs.
O O O X X O X O

A $\frac{3}{5}$ C $\frac{5}{8}$

B $\frac{5}{3}$ D $\frac{3}{8}$

14. Last year 6 out of 8 days were sunny. Which ratio compares sunny days to total days?

F 6 to 8   H $\frac{6}{8}$

G 6:8   J 6 to 14

SKILL 2 — EQUAL RATIOS

The picture can be used to show **equal ratios** that compare squares to circles.

Just as with fractions, ratios can be written in simplest form. $\frac{2}{3}$ is in simplest form.

You can find ratios equal to a given ratio by multiplying or dividing both quantities of a ratio by the same nonzero number.

$$\frac{squares}{circles} = \frac{8}{12} = \frac{6}{9} = \frac{4}{6} = \frac{2}{3}$$

Example 1

Use multiplication to find four ratios equal to the ratio 1 inch to 5 miles.

		1 × 2	1 × 3	1 × 4	1 × 5
Inches	1	2	3	4	5
Miles	5	10	15	20	25
		5 × 2	5 × 3	5 × 4	5 × 5

Example 2

Use multiplication or division to find five ratios equal to the ratio 36 students to 24 adults.

		36 × 2	36 ÷ 2	36 ÷ 12	36 × 3	36 ÷ 6
Students	36	72	18	3	108	6
Adults	24	48	12	2	72	4
		24 × 2	24 ÷ 2	24 ÷ 12	24 × 3	24 ÷ 6

GUIDED PRACTICE

1. Nine pounds of trail mix costs $15. Find two equal ratios.

$$\frac{9}{15} = \frac{9 \times 2}{15 \times 2} = \boxed{}$$ $$\frac{9}{15} = \frac{9 \div 3}{15 \div 3} = \boxed{}$$

For each ratio given, find three equal ratios.

2. $\dfrac{2 \text{ miles}}{8 \text{ minutes}} = $ _____

3. $\dfrac{1 \text{ student}}{3 \text{ students}} = $ _____

4. $\dfrac{5 \text{ pencils}}{1.25 \text{ dollars}} = $ _____

5. $\dfrac{12 \text{ hits}}{50 \text{ at bats}} = $ _____

NOW YOU TRY IT!

Complete each table to show equal ratios.

1.

Tablespoons cocoa	3	6	9				21
Ounces milk	8			32	40	48	

2.

Stickers	50	25				1
Dollars	10.00		2.00	1.00	0.40	

Find three ratios equal to the given ratio.

3. $\dfrac{3 \text{ picture postcards}}{75 \text{ cents}} =$ _____

4. $\dfrac{28 \text{ days}}{4 \text{ weeks}} =$ _____ **5.** $\dfrac{3 \text{ wins}}{6 \text{ games}} =$ _____

6. $\dfrac{12 \text{ inches}}{1 \text{ foot}} =$ _____ **7.** $\dfrac{55 \text{ miles}}{1 \text{ hour}} =$ _____

8. $\dfrac{100 \text{ senators}}{50 \text{ states}} =$ _____

Problem Solving

Alaska has about 110 people per 100 square miles. Answer each question.

9. Is this more or less than 1 person per square mile? _____

10. Write two ratios equal to the ratio $\dfrac{110}{100}$. _____

A LITTLE SOMETHING DIFFERENT...

Make equal ratios by folding paper.

a. Fold a strip of paper into halves. Then fold again into fourths. Fold again into eighths. Open up your sheet. Using the folded sheet, write three equivalent fractions.

_____

b. Take another strip of paper the same size as the first. Fold it into thirds. Fold it again in half to show sixths. Using the folded sheet, write two equivalent fractions.

_____

c. Compare the sheets. Complete the chart.

Halves	Fourths	Thirds	Sixths	Eighths
$\frac{1}{2}$				
$\frac{2}{2}$			$\frac{6}{6}$	
	$\frac{1}{4}$			
	$\frac{3}{4}$			
		$\frac{1}{3}$		
		$\frac{2}{3}$		

 # RATES AND UNIT RATES

A ratio that compares quantities that have two different units is called a **rate**. A **unit rate** compares a quantity with *one unit* of the other quantity. Two examples of unit rates are $.25 per ounce $\left(\frac{\$.25}{1\ oz}\right)$ and 55 miles per hour $\left(\frac{55\ mi}{1\ h}\right)$.

Example 1

Is the ratio $\frac{700\ words}{3\ pages}$ a rate? Is it a unit rate?

The ratio is a rate because the units, words and pages, are different.

It is *not* a unit rate because the comparison is not to 1 page.

Example 2

Find three rates equal to $\frac{\$3}{6\ caramel\ apples}$. Find the unit rate.

Make a table of equal ratios.

The unit rate compares the cost in dollars to 1 apple.

	3 × 2	3 ÷ 3	3 ÷ 6
Cost in dollars	3	6	1	0.50
Apples	6	12	2	1
	6 × 2	6 ÷ 3	6 ÷ 6

Three rates equal to
$\frac{\$3}{6\ caramel\ apples}$
are $\frac{\$6}{12}$, $\frac{\$1}{2}$, and $\frac{\$.50}{1}$.

The unit rate, $\frac{\$.50}{1\ apple}$, may be written as $.50 per apple. This is an example of a **unit price** because it shows the price of one unit of the item.

GUIDED PRACTICE
....

Is the ratio a rate? Write *yes* or *no* and tell why.

1. 5 circles to 2 circles _____ _____.

2. 365 days per year _____ _____.

Is the rate a unit rate? Write *yes* or *no*.

3. $\frac{20\ students}{5\ groups}$ _____
4. $\frac{250\ calories}{3\ servings}$ _____

5. 25 miles per gallon _____
6. $\frac{36\ inches}{3\ feet}$ _____

7. 12 eggs in a dozen _____
8. 8 ounces in a cup _____

9. $\frac{\$9.00}{1\ h}$ _____
10. $8.50 for each person _____

11. $85.00 for 10 people _____
12. 1 book every 2 weeks _____

NOW YOU TRY IT!

Is the ratio a rate? Write *yes* or *no*.

1. 5 gallons in 10 minutes _____   2. 3 teaspoons to 1 teaspoon _____

3. 20 quarters in $5.00 _____   4. 1 car wash every 15 minutes _____

5. 3 daisies for $1.00 _____   6. $20.00 out of every $50.00 _____

Is the rate a unit rate? Write *yes* or *no*. If not, write the rate as a unit rate.

7. 3 weeks per year _____

8. $4.50 for 2 pounds _____

9. $10 for 5 books _____

10. 15 minutes for each quarter _____

11. 7.5¢ per ounce _____

12. $\frac{72 \text{ pages}}{6 \text{ days}}$ _____

13. Every 3 days, Miguel has a total of 90 minutes of softball practice. Give three more rates that describe 90 minutes to 3 days. _____

Problem Solving

Which vehicle has a mileage rate equal to each of the following? Use the chart for exercises 14 through 17.

14. $\frac{100 \text{ mi}}{5 \text{ gal}}$ _____

15. $\frac{100 \text{ mi}}{4 \text{ gal}}$ _____

16. $\frac{60 \text{ mi}}{4 \text{ gal}}$ _____

17. $\frac{60 \text{ mi}}{2 \text{ gal}}$ _____

Gas Mileage of Passenger Vehicles	
Vehicle Type	**Gas Mileage**
Compact car	30 mi/gal
Mid-sized car	25 mi/gal
Mini-van	20 mi/gal
Sport utility	15 mi/gal

TEST PREP

18. Which ratio is a unit rate?

   A 2 mi in 3 h   **C** $7 to $1

   B 3 lb for $2   **D** 30 mi per h

19. Which ratio is equal to $\frac{24}{36}$?

   F $\frac{36}{24}$ **H** $\frac{6}{3}$

   G $\frac{3}{2}$ **J** $\frac{2}{3}$

MEANING OF PROPORTION

Two equal ratios form a **proportion**. Both ratios in a proportion must use the same units. For example, $\frac{1}{2} = \frac{3}{6}$ is a proportion.

Example 1

Do $\frac{4}{5}$ and $\frac{12}{15}$ form a proportion?

$\frac{4}{5} \overset{?}{=} \frac{12}{15}$ $\begin{array}{l}\leftarrow 4 \times 3 = 12 \\ \leftarrow 5 \times 3 = 15\end{array}$ Multiply both terms of one ratio by the same number and get the second ratio. Because the ratios are equal, they do form a proportion.

Example 2

A grocery store sells three oranges for $.49 and a bag of a dozen oranges for $2.00. Are these price rates equal?

Make a table of equal ratios to find the cost of a dozen (12) oranges at the rate of 3 for $.49.

Oranges	3	6	9	12
Dollars	0.49	0.98	1.47	1.96

$\frac{3 \text{ oranges}}{\$.49} = \frac{12 \text{ oranges}}{\$1.96}$, less than the $2.00 for a bag of a dozen.

The prices are not equal rates. They do not form a proportion.

GUIDED PRACTICE

Do $\frac{72}{24}$ and $\frac{8}{3}$ form a proportion?

1. What do you divide 72 by to get 8? _____

2. What do you divide 24 by to get 3? _____

3. Do the ratios form a proportion? Why or why not?

_____

_____

Do the ratios form a proportion? Write *yes* or *no*.

4. $\frac{21}{3} \overset{?}{=} \frac{7}{1}$ 5. $\frac{4}{9} \overset{?}{=} \frac{16}{27}$ 6. $\frac{8}{9} \overset{?}{=} \frac{48}{54}$ 7. $\frac{30}{10} \overset{?}{=} \frac{5}{6}$

_____   _____   _____   _____

8. $\frac{5 \text{ boys}}{4 \text{ girls}} = \frac{20 \text{ girls}}{25 \text{ boys}}$ is not true. Use this information to write a proportion.

_____

Do the ratios form a proportion? Write *yes* or *no*.

1. $\dfrac{7}{15} \stackrel{?}{=} \dfrac{28}{60}$ _____

2. $\dfrac{24}{6} \stackrel{?}{=} \dfrac{12}{3}$ _____

3. $\dfrac{36}{42} \stackrel{?}{=} \dfrac{6}{8}$ _____

4. $\dfrac{6}{13} \stackrel{?}{=} \dfrac{18}{36}$ _____

5. $\dfrac{9}{10} \stackrel{?}{=} \dfrac{54}{60}$ _____

6. $\dfrac{64}{8} \stackrel{?}{=} \dfrac{8}{2}$ _____

7. $\dfrac{5}{9} \stackrel{?}{=} \dfrac{55}{90}$ _____

8. $\dfrac{33}{48} \stackrel{?}{=} \dfrac{11}{16}$ _____

9. $\dfrac{2}{78} \stackrel{?}{=} \dfrac{1}{39}$ _____

10. $\dfrac{15}{75} \stackrel{?}{=} \dfrac{1}{4}$ _____

11. $\dfrac{20}{25} \stackrel{?}{=} \dfrac{4}{5}$ _____

12. $\dfrac{0.5}{2} \stackrel{?}{=} \dfrac{1.0}{4}$ _____

Problem Solving

13. Complete the table of equal ratios for the Pep Club's Lemonade Sale.

Cups sold	450					10	5	1
Profit in dollars	90							

14. What does the ratio for 10 cups sold tell you? _____

15. Write a proportion that gives the unit rate for a cup of lemonade. _____

16. Write a proportion that could be used to find the profit if 300 cups of lemonade are sold. _____

 ## LITTLE SOMETHING DIFFERENT...

Find out which store has the best price for a dozen apples.

a. Complete the price chart. Find the price for a dozen apples at each store.

b. Rank each store's price from 1 to 4 as least expensive to most expensive.

Store	Price	Price/ Dozen	Rank
A	2 apples for $.42		
B	3 apples for $.75		
C	4 apples for $1.05		
D	6 apples for $1.06		

 # CROSS PRODUCTS IN PROPORTIONS

In a proportion, the **cross products** are equal. The cross products are the results of multiplying the numbers in the proportion as shown at the right.

Since the cross products are equal, we know that $\frac{5}{6} = \frac{15}{18}$.

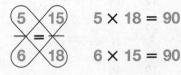

$5 \times 18 = 90$

$6 \times 15 = 90$

Example 1

Do the ratios form a proportion?

$\frac{3}{5} \overset{?}{=} \frac{12}{20}$

$3 \times 20 = 60$

$5 \times 12 = 60$

The cross products are equal,

So $\frac{3}{5} = \frac{12}{20}$.

Example 2

Do the ratios form a proportion?

$\frac{40}{60} \overset{?}{=} \frac{8}{10}$

$40 \times 10 = 400$

$60 \times 8 = 480$

The cross products are not equal, so $\frac{40}{60} \neq \frac{8}{10}$. (Recall that the symbol $\neq$ means *is not equal to*.)

GUIDED PRACTICE

Use the cross products to decide whether the ratios form a proportion. Write = or ≠ .

1. $\frac{4}{5} \overset{?}{=} \frac{2}{3}$

   $4 \times 3 = 12$

   $5 \times 2 = 10$

   $\frac{4}{5} \bigcirc \frac{2}{3}$

2. $\frac{10}{50} \overset{?}{=} \frac{2}{10}$

   $10 \times 10 = 100$

   $50 \times 2 = 100$

   $\frac{10}{50} \bigcirc \frac{2}{10}$

3. $\frac{9}{12} \overset{?}{=} \frac{6}{8}$

   $9 \times 8 = 72$

   $12 \times 6 = 72$

   $\frac{9}{12} \bigcirc \frac{6}{8}$

Use the table at the right.

4. For which two teachers are the ratios of boys to girls equal?

   _____

Class Enrollment		
Teacher	Boys	Girls
Ms. Hong	14	16
Mr. Muñoz	18	12
Mrs. Bruno	12	8
Mr. Ryan	15	8

Do the ratios form a proportion? Write *yes* or *no*.

1. $\frac{6}{12} \overset{?}{=} \frac{12}{14}$ _____

2. $\frac{3}{20} \overset{?}{=} \frac{2}{10}$ _____

3. $\frac{20}{12} \overset{?}{=} \frac{25}{15}$ _____

4. $\frac{27}{6} \overset{?}{=} \frac{36}{8}$ _____

5. $\frac{13}{11} \overset{?}{=} \frac{24}{20}$ _____

6. $\frac{3}{4} \overset{?}{=} \frac{15}{20}$ _____

7. $\frac{10}{4} \overset{?}{=} \frac{45}{20}$ _____

8. $\frac{15}{10} \overset{?}{=} \frac{3}{2}$ _____

9. $\frac{12}{21} \overset{?}{=} \frac{16}{28}$ _____

10. $\frac{3}{24} \overset{?}{=} \frac{4}{32}$ _____

11. $\frac{12}{20} \overset{?}{=} \frac{4}{7}$ _____

12. $\frac{2}{9} \overset{?}{=} \frac{5}{22}$ _____

13. $\frac{2 \text{ tsp}}{7 \text{ gal}} \overset{?}{=} \frac{6 \text{ tsp}}{21 \text{ gal}}$ _____

14. $\frac{12 \text{ cm}}{20 \text{ g}} \overset{?}{=} \frac{15 \text{ g}}{25 \text{ cm}}$ _____

15. $\frac{\$14}{3 \text{ hr}} \overset{?}{=} \frac{\$84}{18 \text{ hr}}$ _____

16. $\frac{27 \text{ lb}}{\$21} \overset{?}{=} \frac{14 \text{ lb}}{\$18}$ _____

17. $\frac{15 \text{ sec}}{21 \text{ sec}} \overset{?}{=} \frac{10 \text{ in.}}{15 \text{ in.}}$ _____

18. $\frac{6 \text{ ft}}{13 \text{ gal}} \overset{?}{=} \frac{7 \text{ ft}}{14 \text{ gal}}$ _____

19. $\frac{5 \text{ sec}}{9 \text{ m}} \overset{?}{=} \frac{20 \text{ sec}}{45 \text{ m}}$ _____

20. $\frac{1 \text{hr}}{7 \text{ g}} \overset{?}{=} \frac{7 \text{ hr}}{49 \text{ g}}$ _____

21. $\frac{32 \text{ min}}{50 \text{ mi}} \overset{?}{=} \frac{63 \text{ min}}{100 \text{ mi}}$ _____

Problem Solving

Use the data given in the table.

Runner	Distance	Time
Joyce	100 m	12 sec
Larry	500 m	55 sec
Tanya	10 m	1 sec
Alan	200 m	24 sec

22. Which two students ran at the same rate?

_____

23. Larry ran 200 meters in 16 seconds. Did he run 200 meters at the same rate that he ran 500 meters? _____

24. At the rate given for 10 meters, how long would it take Tanya to run 100 meters? _____

25. If Joyce ran at the same rate shown for 48 seconds, how for would she have gone? _____

TEST PREP

26. What is the cross product for this proportion: $\frac{8}{5} = \frac{24}{15}$?

    A 120   **C** 192

    B 75   **D** 110

27. Which shows a true proportion?

    F $\frac{5}{7} = \frac{10}{15}$ **H** $\frac{22}{6} = \frac{11}{2}$

    G $\frac{4}{3} = \frac{12}{16}$ **J** $\frac{18}{12} = \frac{3}{2}$

SOLVING PROPORTIONS USING CROSS PRODUCTS

To **solve a proportion**, you must find the missing number that makes the proportion true. You can use cross products to find this missing value.

Example 1

Use cross products to find the missing number: $\frac{\square}{21} = \frac{3}{7}$

$\square \times 7 = 21 \times 3$ If the proportion is true, its cross products must be equal.

$\square \times 7 = 63$ Multiply: $21 \times 3 = 63$.

$63 \div 7 = 9$ Use division to undo multiplication.

So, the value of the missing number is 9.

Example 2

Find the unit rate equal to $12 for 4 pounds.

$\frac{12 \text{ dollars}}{4 \text{ pounds}} = \frac{n \text{ dollars}}{1 \text{ pound}}$ The unit rate is an equal ratio that compares the cost, n dollars, to one pound.

$12 \times 1 = 4 \times n$ Write the cross products.

$12 = 4 \times n$ Multiply: 12×1.

$\frac{12}{4} = \frac{4 \times n}{4}$ Use division to undo multiplication.

$3 = n$ So, $\frac{12}{4} = \frac{3}{1}$.

The unit rate, or unit price, is 3 dollars for 1 pound.

GUIDED PRACTICE

Use cross products to solve each proportion.

1. $\frac{2}{8} = \frac{1.5}{n}$ 2. $\frac{6}{10} = \frac{n}{12}$ 3. $\frac{5}{n} = \frac{6}{36}$

    $2 \times n = $ _____ $\times$ _____ $10 \times n = $ _____ $\times$ _____ $6 \times n = $ _____ $\times$ _____

    $2 \times n = $ _____   _____ $= $ _____   _____ $=$ _____

        $n = $ _____ $n = $ _____ $n = $ _____

4. Write a proportion to find the unit rate   miles $\rightarrow \dfrac{\square}{\square} = \dfrac{n}{1}$ $\leftarrow$
   for 35 miles on 10 liters of gasoline.   liters $\rightarrow$

    Write cross products. _____ $\times$ _____ $=$ _____ $\times$ _____

    Solve the proportion. $n = $ _____

    Write the unit rate. _____

_____

NOW YOU TRY IT!

Solve each proportion.

1. $\frac{2}{8} = \frac{n}{20}$

   _____ = _____

   _____ = _____

   $n =$ _____

2. $\frac{15}{5} = \frac{6}{n}$

   _____ = _____

   _____ = _____

   $n =$ _____

3. $\frac{n}{4} = \frac{6}{3}$

   _____ = _____

   _____ = _____

   $n =$ _____

4. $\frac{4}{5} = \frac{8}{n}$

   _____

5. $\frac{12}{8} = \frac{6}{n}$

   _____

6. $\frac{n}{8} = \frac{3}{4}$

   _____

7. $\frac{20}{8} = \frac{n}{2}$

   _____

8. $\frac{4}{n} = \frac{2}{7}$

   _____

9. $\frac{n}{15} = \frac{2}{6}$

   _____

10. $\frac{2}{n} = \frac{8}{4}$

    _____

11. $\frac{n}{8} = \frac{20}{40}$

    _____

12. $\frac{8}{36} = \frac{n}{9}$

    _____

13. $\frac{30}{3} = \frac{n}{2}$

    _____

14. $\frac{3}{7} = \frac{12}{n}$

    _____

15. $\frac{n}{9} = \frac{5}{4.5}$

    _____

Problem Solving

Find the unit price.

16. $1.20 for 24 ounces of juice. _____ **per ounce**

17. $12 for 8 pounds of peanuts. _____ **per pound**

18. 4 quarts of milk cost $3.88. _____ **per quart**

19. 12 yards of yarn cost $12.00. _____ **per yard**

20. 6 hours of studio time cost $624.00. _____ **per hour**

21. 12 liters of juice cost $21.00. _____ **per liter**

 A LITTLE SOMETHING DIFFERENT...

**Solve the riddle by finding the missing number in the proportions.
Match the number to the letter in the chart.**

What is filled with holes and still holds water?

1	2	3	4	5
R	W	O	E	N
6	7	8	9	10
G	U	S	P	A

1. $\frac{2}{5} = \frac{4}{?}$ _____

2. $\frac{4}{5} = \frac{?}{10}$ _____

3. $\frac{3}{4} = \frac{?}{12}$ _____

4. $\frac{1}{6} = \frac{?}{18}$ _____

5. $\frac{?}{8} = \frac{10}{16}$ _____

6. $\frac{2}{5} = \frac{?}{15}$ _____

7. $\frac{1}{2} = \frac{2}{?}$ _____

Answer: ___ ___ ___ ___ ___ ___ ___
          1   2   3   4   5   6   7

TEST PREP

Circle each correct answer.

1. Find the cross product. $\frac{3}{8} = \frac{6}{16}$

   A 18   **C** 48

   B 42   **D** 128

2. Which shows a proportion?

   F $\frac{20}{32} = \frac{5}{8}$ **H** $\frac{6}{5} = \frac{10}{12}$

   G $\frac{3}{4} = \frac{4}{3}$ **J** $\frac{15}{30} = \frac{1}{3}$

3. Which ratio **does not** show 7 students to 10 adults?

   A $\frac{10}{7}$ **C** $\frac{7}{10}$

   B 7 to 10   **D** 7:10

4. Which ratio forms a proportion with $\frac{18}{21}$?

   F $\frac{1}{2}$ **H** $\frac{2}{3}$

   G $\frac{3}{4}$ **J** $\frac{4}{5}$

5. Solve: $\frac{6}{9} = \frac{x}{30}$.

   A 45   **C** 180

   B 30   **D** 20

6. Which is a unit rate?

   F $\frac{12 \text{ limes}}{\$1}$ **H** $\frac{\$1}{\$10}$

   G $\frac{2 \text{ L}}{\$1.19}$ **J** $\frac{8 \text{ tokens}}{\$10}$

7. Which ratio forms a proportion with $\frac{5}{6}$?

   A $\frac{6}{5}$ **C** $\frac{20}{24}$

   B $\frac{20}{30}$ **D** $\frac{24}{20}$

8. Which ratio is equal to $\frac{5}{8}$?

   F $\frac{8}{3}$ **H** $\frac{16}{6}$

   G $\frac{16}{40}$ **J** $\frac{45}{72}$

9. Find the cross product: $\frac{3}{4.5} = \frac{6}{9}$.

   A 18   **C** 40.5

   B 27   **D** 2

10. If 24 identical prints cost $5.04, how much does each print cost?

    F $.21   **H** $120.96

    G $2.10   **J** $12

11. What is the ratio of boys to girls in a class of 32 students where 15 are boys?

    A $\frac{17}{32}$ **C** $\frac{17}{15}$

    B $\frac{15}{17}$ **D** $\frac{32}{15}$

SOMETHING DIFFERENT...

RUNNING A WATER CONSERVATION CAMPAIGN

You are very concerned about people wasting water, especially when the water supply is low. You decide to conduct a campaign to get people to conserve water. Work with a partner. Your job is to create a poster to compare average water use now and how water use can be far better. Your goal is to show how each person can conserve at least 20 gallons of water each day by just being careful. You can do it in many different ways.

Rules for Making Your Poster

1. Use at least one chart on your poster.

2. You may use graphs. They can be very effective! Be sure to label them correctly.

3. You must use ratios and proportions in your calculations.

4. Make your poster very visual. In other words, use charts, graphs, or other devices. That's the way to catch people's eyes!

5. You must show the comparison of wasteful use to an improved use.

6. You must show that at least 20 gal of water can be saved each day by the average person.

Now for some facts. Use as many as you can in your poster.

The Kitchen/Laundry

◊ Washing dishes by hand:
5 gal each time

◊ Washing in a dishwasher: short cycle:
10 gal per load

◊ Washing in a dishwasher, standard cycle: 15 gal per load

◊ Laundry, top-loading washer:
55 gal per load

◊ Laundry, front-loading washer:
20 gal per load

The Bathroom

◊ Brushing teeth with tap running:
2 gal per each time

◊ Brushing teeth with tap on only to rinse: 1/4 gal

◊ Flushing toilet, standard toilet:
5 gal per flush

◊ Toilet, low volume toilet: 1.6 gal per flush

◊ Shower: 56.3 gal for an average 6.3 min shower

◊ Bath: 35 gal

◊ Shaving, open tap: 6 gal

◊ Shaving, full basin: 1 gal

Share your poster with the other members of the class.

SKILL 7 VARIABLES AND EXPRESSIONS

A **variable** is a quantity that can change or vary. Mathematicians use letters to represent variables.

A quantity that does not change is a **constant**.

An **expression** is a mathematical phrase involving constants, variables, and operation symbols. There are different ways to represent different operations. Four examples are shown below.

Addition:	$x + 6$	x is the variable.	6 is the constant.
Subtraction:	$91 - x$	x is the variable.	91 is the constant.
Multiplication:	$3x$ or $3 \times x$	x is the variable.	3 is the constant.
Division:	$12 \div x$ or $\frac{12}{x}$	x is the variable.	12 is the constant.

If you know the values of the variable, you can *evaluate* the expression by replacing the variable with each value. This is known as *substituting a value for the variable.*

Example

Evaluate $2x$ for $x = 4$, 6, and 8.

$2x$ means "2 times x." To evaluate the expression, you need to substitute a value for x.

When $x = 4$, substitute 4 for x: You can make a table to evaluate the expression for multiple values of x.

x	$2x$
4	$2 \times 4 = 8$
6	$2 \times 6 = 12$
8	$2 \times 8 = 16$

So $2x = 8$ when $x = 4$; $2x = 12$ when $x = 6$; and $2x = 16$ when $x = 8$.

GUIDED PRACTICE

1. Evaluate $x + 12$ for $x = 2$, 5, and 10.

   a. Substitute 2 for x. Solve: $2 + 12 =$ _____

   b. Substitute 5 for x. Solve: $5 + 12 =$ _____

   c. Substitute 10 for x. Solve: $10 + 12 =$ _____

2. Evaluate each expression for $x = 2$, 5, and 10.

   a. $6x$ _____ _____ _____

   b. $x - 1$ _____ _____ _____

   c. $50 \div x$ _____ _____ _____

   d. $27 + x$ _____ _____ _____

NOW YOU TRY IT!

1. Complete the table by evaluating each expression for $x = 2$, 3, and 4.

x	$x + 5$	$17 - x$	$9x$	$\frac{144}{x}$	$x \times 7$	x^2	$5x$
2							
3							
4							

2. Complete the table by evaluating each expression for $x = 3$, 5, and 9.

x	$16 + x$	$x - 3$	$12 \times x$	$90 \div x$	$20x$	$100 - x$	$x \div x$
3							
5							
9							

3. Complete the table by evaluating each expression for $x = 2$, 4, and 7.

x	$x + 43$	$30 - x$	$x \times x$	$x \times 10$	$2x$	$\frac{112}{x}$	x^3
2							
4							
7							

TEST PREP

4. Evaluate the expression $\frac{x^2}{5} + 3$ when $x = -5$.

   A -2 **C** $5\frac{3}{5}$

   B $3\frac{1}{3}$ **D** 8

5. What is the value of x?

Number of balls	Number of packages
30	10
72	24
378	126
999	x

   F 228   **H** 333

   G 300   **J** 2997

WRITING EXPRESSIONS

Some words in English can be translated into specific mathematical operations.

Word	Definition	Numerical Expression	Variable Expression
sum	The result of **adding** numbers	$7 + 2$	$8 + x$
difference	The result of **subtracting** numbers	$12 - 3$	$28 - y$
product	The result of **multiplying** numbers	4×16	$8c$
quotient	The result of **dividing** numbers	$81 \div 9$	$\frac{14}{s}$ or $14 \div s$

To translate situations that don't use these words, you need to choose an operation that is appropriate for the situation. It may be easier to choose an operation if you first replace the variable with a number.

Example

Write an expression to answer: What is the quotient of 99 divided by *x*?

Step 1: What operation is being done?   A quotient is the answer when dividing, so use division to write the expression.

Step 2: Use the appropriate sign to write the expression: $99 \div x$ or $\frac{99}{x}$

The expressions $99 \div x$ and $\frac{99}{x}$ shows the quotient of 99 divided by *x*.

GUIDED PRACTICE

1. Write an expression to answer: What is 12 minus *r*?

   a. What operation is being done? _____

   b. Write the expression. _____

2. Write an expression to answer each question.

   a. What is 32 times as big as *y*? _____

   b. What is 24 more than *n*? _____

   c. What is 11 less than *b*? _____

   d. What is *d* divided by 5? _____

   e. What is *g* plus 10? _____

   f. Brian has *p* pencils and bought 4 more.
   How many does he have? _____

Write the phrase as an expression.

1. 12 more than x _____

2. x less than 36 _____

3. one-third of a _____

4. 17 times s _____

5. b multiplied by 5 _____

6. y to the fourth power _____

7. 64 plus k _____

8. u tripled _____

Write an expression to answer each question.

9. What is the product of 82 and g? _____

10. What is the difference between n and 7? _____

11. What is the quotient of 32 and x? _____

12. What is the sum of h and 7? _____

13. What is 31 less than c? _____

14. What is the fifth power of t? _____

15. What is one-eighth of r? _____

Problem Solving

16. Thomas Jefferson became President of the United States in 1801. George Washington became president y years earlier. In what year did George Washington become president? _____

17. A spider has 8 legs. How many legs do s spiders have? _____

A LITTLE SOMETHING DIFFERENT...

With a friend, solve the following expression as quickly as possible.

a. Write your age. _____

b. Multiply by 2. _____

c. Add 16. _____

d. Divide by 2. _____

e. Subtract 8. _____

f. Write an algebraic expression for what took place. Use x for your age. _____

g. Try it with other ages. What happens?

_____

_____

SKILL 9 — USING EQUATIONS

An **equation** is a mathematical sentence that uses an equal sign, =, to show that two expressions are equal. An equation can be either true or false. For example, $13 + 12 = 25$ is true because both sides have the same value. However, $85 - 21 = 82$ is false because both sides of the equation do **not** have the same value.

An equation with a variable can also be true or false, depending on the value of the variable.

Example

Is the equation true for the given value of the variable?

a. $4y = 24$, $y = 6$

$4 \times 6 \overset{?}{=} 24$ Substitute 6 for y.

$24 = 24$ Multiply.

Since both sides of the equation have the same value, the equation is true.

b. $8 + a = 10$, $a = 3$

$8 + a \overset{?}{=} 10$ Substitute 3 for a.

$11 \neq 10$ Add.

Since both sides of the equation do **not** have the same value, the equation is false.

GUIDED PRACTICE

1. Is the equation true for the given value of the variable: $28 \div x = 7$, $x = 4$?

   a. What value will you substitute for x? _____

   b. Rewrite the equation, substituting for x. _____

   c. Is the equation you wrote in Item b true or false? _____

2. Is the equation true for the given value of the variable?

   a. $k + 65 = 100$, $x = 25$ _____

   b. $56 - j = 40$, $j = 20$ _____

   c. $2w = 60$, $w = 30$ _____

   d. $7 \times b = 49$, $b = 7$ _____

   e. $40 + q = 60$, $q = 25$ _____

....

Is the equation true for the given value of the variable?

1. $x + 5 = 17, x = 22$ _____
2. $3 - y = 1, y = 2$ _____
3. $4x = 24, x = 6$ _____
4. $g - 7 = 11, g = 18$ _____
5. $s \div 7 = 3, s = 21$ _____
6. $u + 12 = 31, u = 20$ _____
7. $h - 13 = 21, h = 34$ _____
8. $64 \div n = 16, n = 8$ _____
9. $20 \times t = 300, t = 160$ _____
10. $18 - c = 10, c = 8$ _____
11. $m + 40 = 92, m = 50$ _____
12. $x \div 5 = 15, x = 75$ _____
13. $3k = 27, k = 9$ _____
14. $z - 9 = 61, z = 52$ _____
15. $12 + v = 21, v = 7$ _____
16. $5w = 20, w = 4$ _____
17. $n - 6 = 24, n = 18$ _____
18. $k \div 8 = 9, k = 56$ _____
19. $m + 12 = 61, m = 49$ _____
20. $j + 17 = 86, j = 79$ _____

Problem Solving

Write an equation for each situation.

21. Jim had 18 CDs. He bought x more. Then he had 21 CDs. _____

22. Rolando baked 4 loaves of bread, each weighing w oz.
The total weight was 80 oz. _____

23. Veronica had m marbles. She gave 5 to Marco.
She had 12 marbles left. _____

24. The lunch period at Eisenhower School is normally
35 minutes. On Thursday, students were given an extra
t minutes, so they had 55 minutes for lunch. _____

25. Ellwood had 8 harmonicas. On Saturday he bought m
more. He now has 13 harmonicas. _____

TEST PREP

26. Solve: $m + 12 = 61$

    A 73 **C** 49

    B 61 **D** 5.08

27. Which equation matches the situation: Jill has three dollars. She buys x number of oranges. Each orange cost 50 cents.

    F $\frac{0.50}{x} = 3.00$ **H** $0.50 - x = 3.00$

    G $0.50 + x = 3.00$ **J** $0.50(x) = 3.00$

SOLVING EQUATIONS

Sometimes you need to find the exact value that will make an equation true. This is known as *solving the equation.*

Think of equations as questions where the variable is read as "what number?" For example, $a + 3 = 10$ can be read as "What number plus 3 equals 10?" Use mental math to answer the question.

Example

Solve $y - 8 = 7$.

Step 1: Read as: "What number minus 8 equals 7?" $y - 8 = 7$
Step 2: Use mental math. $15 - 8 = 7$
Step 3: Check to see that the equation is true. $7 = 7$
In the equation $y - 8 = 7$, y is equal to 15.

GUIDED PRACTICE

1. Solve $a + 5 = 12$.
   a. What number plus 5 equals 12? _____ so a = _____
   b. Show that the equation is true. _____

2. Solve $3x = 18$.
   a. What number times 3 equals 18? _____ so x = _____
   b. Show that the equation is true. _____

3. Solve $m \div 3 = 20$.
   a. What number divided by 3 = 20? _____ so m = _____
   b. Show that the equation is true. _____

Solve each equation.

4. $y + 15 = 50$ y = _____   5. $b - 4 = 8$ b = _____

6. $\frac{w}{2} = 6$ w = _____   7. $3 \times c = 27$ c = _____

8. $28 - p = 19$ p = _____   9. $t + 8 = 26$ t = _____

10. $11s = 110$ s = _____   11. $81 \div k = 9$ k = _____

12. $17 + r = 40$ r = _____   13. $h \div 3 = 12$ h = _____

Find the given value of x that makes the equation true.

1. $\frac{x}{7} = 4$; $x = 28, 35, 42,$ or 49

   _____

2. $x - 6 = 13$; $x = 18, 19, 20,$ or 21

   _____

3. $5x = 45$; $x = 6, 7, 8,$ or 9

   _____

4. $x + 8 = 17$; $x = 8, 9, 10,$ or 11

   _____

Solve the equation.

5. $x + 7 = 30$ _____

6. $m - 10 = 7$ _____

7. $\frac{s}{8} = 13$ _____

8. $11t = 88$ _____

9. $d - 12 = 69$ _____

10. $21 + g = 42$ _____

11. $7u = 35$ _____

12. $n \div 7 = 8$ _____

13. $b - 7 = 24$ _____

Problem Solving

Write an equation for each situation and then solve the equation.

14. The top three best-selling albums of all time are Michael Jackson's *Thriller* (24 million copies), Fleetwood Mac's *Rumours* (17 million copies), and Boston's *Boston* (*b* million copies). The three albums sold a combined total of 56 million copies. How many million copies of *Boston* were sold?

    _____

15. The main audience section of the Mel Mello Center for the Arts has 9 rows of *c* chairs. There are 126 chairs all together. How many chairs are in each row?

    _____

 LITTLE SOMETHING DIFFERENT...

Solve the puzzle. Write the solution to the equations on the blanks provided.

How tall is Africa's highest peak, Mount Kilimanjaro?

a. $24 - x = 23$ b. $m - 6 = 3$ c. $36 \div y = 12$

d. $\frac{28}{n} = 7$ e. $42c = 42$

_____ _____ , _____ _____ _____ feet
  a   b   c   d   e

TEST PREP
EXPRESSIONS
Please circle your responses directly on the test.

1. Rhonda has u CDs and each of her CDs has 10 songs. What is the total number of songs in her collection?

  A $10 + u$ **C** $100u$

  B $10u$ **D** $10 \div u$

2. What value makes the following equation true? $4y = 36$.

  F 8   **H** 9

  G 40   **J** 32

3. Solve: $p - 11 = 38$

  A 27   **C** 60

  B 49   **D** 16

4. A school bus has 2 benches in each row. There are 42 benches all together. How many rows are there?

  F 2   **H** 42

  G 21   **J** 84

5. If $x = 8$, what is $56 \div x$?

  A 9   **C** 7

  B 48   **D** 64

6. Write the expression to answer the question. Max is 48 in. tall. Nell is n in. shorter than Max. How tall is Nell?

  F $48 + n$ **H** $n - 48$

  G $48 \div n$ **J** $48 - n$

7. Solve: $19 + t = 43$.

  A 24   **C** 62

  B 21   **D** 42

8. What is the value of x?

Number of Days	Number of acres
1	90
2	180
3	270
4	x

  F 450   **H** 360

  G 180   **J** 540

9. Solve: p cubed, if $p = 6$.

  A 216   **C** 18

  B 36   **D** 9

10. Write an equation:

Each of the 50 United States has s U.S. Senators. There are 100 U.S. Senators all together.

  F $100 - 50 = s$ **H** $50s = 100$

  G $50 = 100s$ **J** $100 \times 50 = s$

SOMETHING DIFFERENT...
FASTER THAN A SPEEDING BULLET—WELL, NOT QUITE!

Formulas can be very handy. When you know some of the
values and are missing one, you can turn the formula around to
help you. Think about the formula for finding distance.

$$\text{Distance} = \text{rate} \times \text{time}$$
$$D = rt$$

To find distance all you do is multiply the rate times the time.
If you know the distance and you want to find either rate
or time you can rewrite the formula in the following way.

To solve for rate, solve the
formula for r.

$D = rt$
$\frac{D}{t} = r$

To solve for time, solve the
equation for t.

$D = rt$
$\frac{D}{r} = t$

Use the formula. Find the missing value. If you see the word
"about" you can round your answer to the nearest whole number.

	Means of Transportation	D	r	t
1.	Train	145 mi	70 mph	About ____ hr
2.	Bike	35 mi	_____ mph	1.4 hr
3.	Car driving in traffic	5 mi	12 mph	About_____min
4.	Car on the Freeway, no traffic	About _____ mi	60 mph	20 min
5.	Airplane	8,465 mi	About_____ mph	3 hr 15 min
6.	Horse and Buggy	35 mi	20 mph	____ hr _____ min
7.	Roller Coaster	1.4 mi	70 mph	About _____ min
8.	Subway	15 mi	60 mph	_____ min
9.	Sail Boat	43 mi	4.7 mph	About _____ hr
10.	Motor Boat	43 mi	12 mph	About ___ hr _____ min

24

SKILL 11 — MEANING OF PERCENT

A **percent** is a ratio that makes a comparison to 100. The meaning of percent is hundredths. So 80% is 80 hundredths, or $\frac{80}{100}$.

Example 1

What percent (%) of the figure is shaded?

45 out of 100 squares, or 45 hundredths of the squares are shaded.

$\frac{45}{100} = 45\%$, so **45%** of the figure is shaded.

Example 2

What percent of the circle is shaded?

3 out of 4 of the sections of the circle are shaded. Find a ratio equal to $\frac{3}{4}$ with a denominator of 100.

Then write the percent.

$\frac{3}{4} = \frac{3 \times 25}{4 \times 25} = \frac{75}{100} = 75\%$, so **75%** of the circle is shaded.

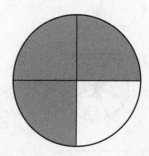

GUIDED PRACTICE

Give the percent of each figure that is shaded.

1.    2.    3. 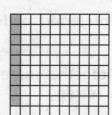   4.

_____   _____   _____   _____

5.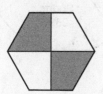

$\frac{1}{2} = \frac{\boxed{}}{100}$

$\frac{1}{2} = $ _____

6.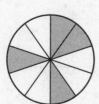

$\frac{4}{10} = \frac{\boxed{}}{100}$

$\frac{4}{10} = $ _____

7.

$\frac{1}{4} = \frac{\boxed{}}{100}$

$\frac{1}{4} = $ _____

8.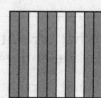

$\frac{7}{10} = \frac{\boxed{}}{100}$

$\frac{7}{10} = $ _____

NOW YOU TRY IT!

What percent of the figure is shaded?

1.

   _____

2.

   _____

3.

   _____

4.

   _____

5.

   _____

6.

   _____

7.

   _____

8.

   _____

9.

   _____

Problem Solving

Solve each problem using the circle graph.

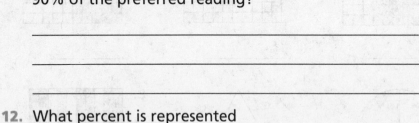

10. What percent of the preferred reading is humor or mystery books? _____

11. What types of books together represent 90% of the preferred reading?

    _____

    _____

    _____

12. What percent is represented by the entire circle? _____

13. What percent is represented by sports or biography? _____

TEST PREP

14. What percent of the figure is shaded?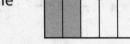

    A 0.4   **C** 40%

    B $\frac{2}{5}$ **D** 60%

15. Which ratio is equal to $\frac{16}{20}$?

    F $\frac{3}{5}$ **H** $\frac{5}{4}$

    G $\frac{4}{5}$ **J** $\frac{6}{10}$

Preferred Reading (circle graph)
- Biography 4%
- Romance 6%
- Animals 10%
- Humor 14%
- Sports 26%
- Mystery 40%

26   © by Pearson Education, Inc., publishing as Pearson Prentice Hall

 **SKILL 12**

FRACTIONS, DECIMALS, PERCENT

Fractions, decimals, and percents all describe parts of a whole.

- To convert a fraction to a percent, write an equal fraction with a denominator of 100. You might want to use a proportion to do this.

- To convert a decimal to a percent, multiply the decimal by 100 and write the percent symbol. Remember, to multiply by 100, you can simply move the decimal point two places to the right.

Example 1

Write 15% as a fraction in simplest form and as a decimal.

Fraction: $15\% = \frac{15}{100} = \frac{15 \div 5}{100 \div 5} = \frac{3}{20}$ Decimal: $15\% = \frac{15}{100} = 0.15$

Example 2

Write $\frac{1}{6}$ as a percent. Round to the nearest tenth.

Write a proportion using $\frac{1}{6}$ and a $\frac{1}{6} = \frac{x}{100}$
fraction with a denominator of 100.

Find the cross products. $6x = 100$

Divide both sides by 6. $x = 100 \div 6$

                                        $x \approx 16.7$

Recall that the symbol $\approx$ means *is approximately equal to.*
So, $\frac{1}{6} \approx 16.7\%$

GUIDED PRACTICE

Write each percent as a fraction in simplest form and as a decimal.

1. $67\% = \frac{67}{100}$ _____; _____   2. $8\% = \frac{8}{100}$ _____; _____

Write each decimal as a percent.

3. $0.6 = 0.60 =$ _____   4. $0.59 =$ _____   5. $0.231 =$ _____

Solve each proportion. Then write the percent.

6. $\frac{7}{10} = \frac{x}{100}$ 7. $\frac{5}{8} = \frac{x}{100}$ 8. $\frac{2}{3} = \frac{x}{100}$

   $x =$ _____ $x =$ _____ $x \approx$ _____

   $\frac{7}{10} =$ _____ $\frac{5}{8} =$ _____ $\frac{2}{3} \approx$ _____

Convert each percent to a fraction in lowest terms and to a decimal.

1. 80%

   Fraction: _____

   Decimal: _____

2. 25%

   Fraction: _____

   Decimal: _____

3. 3%

   Fraction: _____

   Decimal: _____

4. 75%

   Fraction: _____

   Decimal: _____

5. 16%

   Fraction: _____

   Decimal: _____

6. 94%

   Fraction: _____

   Decimal: _____

Convert each fraction or decimal to a percent.
Round to the nearest tenth of a percent if necessary.

7. $\frac{3}{10}$ _____

8. $\frac{37}{50}$ _____

9. $\frac{18}{20}$ _____

10. $\frac{1}{2}$ _____

11. $\frac{4}{5}$ _____

12. $\frac{93}{100}$ _____

13. 0.43 _____

14. 0.01 _____

15. 0.74 _____

Problem Solving

The table at the right shows what part of her allowance each girl saves.

16. Who saves the greatest percent of her allowance? _____

17. Who saves the smallest percent of her allowance? _____

18. Which girls save the same percent? _____

Savings Rate	
Lindy	$\frac{1}{5}$
Sonia	16%
Annie	0.25
Gena	20%
Mari	$\frac{1}{10}$

 **A LITTLE SOMETHING DIFFERENT...**

Create a quick reference for converting between fractions, decimals, and percents.

It's handy to be able to recognize some common conversions of fractions, decimals, and percents. Complete the chart below.

Fraction			$\frac{3}{4}$		
Decimal		0.25			0.2
Percent	50%			$33\frac{1}{3}$%	

SKILL 13 FINDING A PERCENT OF A NUMBER

To find a percent of a number, you can use a proportion, or you can write the percent as a decimal and multiply.

Example

Find 22% of 83.

Proportion Method

Write a proportion. Then find the cross products and solve for *x*.

part → $\frac{x}{83} = \frac{22}{100}$ ← Write the
whole percent as a fraction over 100.

$100x = 1826$

$x = 1826 \div 100$

$x = 18.26$

22% of 83 is 18.26

Equation Method

Change the percent to a decimal and multiply.

$22\% \text{ of } 83 = 0.22 \times 83$

$= 18.26$

22% of 83 is 18.26.

GUIDED PRACTICE

Find 6% of 30 using the indicated method.

1. Write a proportion.

$\frac{x}{30} = \frac{6}{100}$

$100x =$ _____

$x =$ _____

6% of 30 = _____

2. Write an equation.

6% of 30 = _____ × 30

= _____

6% of 30 = _____

Find the percent of each number.

3. 25% of 84

$0.25 \times 84 =$ _____

25% of 84 = _____

4. 10% of 7

$0.1 \times 7 =$ _____

10% of 7 = _____

5. 91% of 37

_____ × _____ = _____

91% of 37 = _____

6. 60% of 45

$0.6 \times 45 =$ _____

60% of 45 = _____

7. 4.2% of 50

$0.042 \times 50 =$ _____

4.2% of 50 = _____

8. 75% of 160

_____ × 160 = _____

75% of 160 = _____

NOW YOU TRY IT!

Find the percent of each number.

1. 50% of 66 = _____
2. 25% of 72 = _____
3. 40% of 180 = _____
4. $33\frac{1}{3}$ % of 123 = _____
5. 54% of 120 = _____
6. 0% of 14 = _____
7. 22% of 96 = _____
8. 4% of 180 = _____
9. 100% of 180 = _____
10. 19.2% of 50 = _____
11. 31.4% of 20 = _____
12. 8.8% of 700 = _____
13. 3.8% of 145 = _____
14. 98.5% of 150 = _____
15. 45% of 75 = _____
16. 1.2% of 200 = _____
17. 75% of 360 = _____
18. 20% of 65 = _____

Solve each problem. Try to find a pattern.

19. 10% of 37 = _____

    37% of 10 = _____
20. 78% of 50 = _____

    50% of 78 = _____
21. 28% of 25 = _____

    25% of 28 = _____
22. 47% of 40 = _____

    40% of 47 = _____

Problem Solving

23. Of the 50 students in Class A, 48% are boys. How many of the students are boys?   _____

24. The basketball team won 68% of the 25 games played. How many games did the team win?   _____

25. Out of 52 weeks, 25% are in winter.   _____

TEST PREP

26. Find 25% of 120.

    A 300

    B 3

    C 480

    D 30

27. Which is the cross product of $\frac{4}{12} = \frac{6}{18}$?

    F 24

    G 42

    H 216

    J 72

NAME _____ DATE _____

 # USING MENTAL MATH TO FIND A PERCENT OF A NUMBER

Some fraction, decimal, and percent conversions that are frequently used are shown in the table. You can use these percents to find others.

$3 \times 25\% = 75\%$, so $75\% = 3 \times \frac{1}{4} = \frac{3}{4}$.

Fraction	Decimal	Percent
$\frac{1}{2}$	0.5	50%
$\frac{1}{3}$	$0.33\frac{1}{3}$	$33\frac{1}{3}\%$
$\frac{1}{4}$	0.25	25%
$\frac{1}{5}$	0.2	20%
$\frac{1}{8}$	$0.12\frac{1}{2}$	$12\frac{1}{2}\%$
$\frac{1}{10}$	0.1	10%

Example 1
Find 25% of 28.

Think: $25\% = \frac{1}{4}$. $\frac{1}{4} \times 28 = \frac{28}{4} = 7$,
so 25% of 28 = 7.

Example 2
Find 60% of 80.

Think: $10\% \times 80 = \frac{1}{10} \times 80 = 8$. Since 60% is $6 \times 10\%$,
multiply the result by 6.

$6 \times 8 = 48$, so 60% of 80 = 48.

Example 3
Find $33\frac{1}{3}\%$ of 240.

Think: $33\frac{1}{3}\% = \frac{1}{3}$. $\frac{1}{3} \times 240 = \frac{240}{3} = 80$, so, $33\frac{1}{3}\%$ of 240 = 80.

GUIDED PRACTICE

Use mental math to find each percent.

1. Find 50% of 300.
   Think: $50\% = \frac{1}{2}$. $\frac{1}{2} \times 300 =$ _____, so 50% of 300 = _____.

2. Find $12\frac{1}{2}\%$ of 24.
   Think: $12\frac{1}{2}\% = \frac{1}{8}$. $\frac{1}{8} \times 24 =$ _____, so $12\frac{1}{2}\%$ of 24 = _____.

3. Find $33\frac{1}{3}\%$ of 15.
   Think: $33\frac{1}{3}\% = \frac{1}{3}$. $\frac{1}{3} \times 15 =$ _____, so $33\frac{1}{3}\%$ of 15 = _____.

4. Find 87% of 10.
   Think: 87% of 10 = 10% of 87 = _____.

5. 20% of 45 = _____
6. $66\frac{2}{3}\%$ of 90 = _____
7. 10% of 53 = _____
8. 75% of 16 = _____
9. 100% of 93 = _____
10. 44% of 50 = _____

© by Pearson Education, Inc., publishing as Pearson Prentice Hall   31

NOW YOU TRY IT!

Use mental math to find each percent of 400.

1. 50% _____
2. 25% _____
3. $37\frac{1}{2}$% _____
4. 5% _____

5. 1% _____
6. 20% _____
7. 80% _____
8. 30% _____

Use mental math to find each percent.

9. 50% of 420 = _____
10. 75% of 80 = _____
11. 10% of 57 = _____

12. 83% of 10 = _____
13. $33\frac{1}{3}$% of 48 = _____
14. 100% of 35 = _____

15. $12\frac{1}{2}$% of 40 = _____
16. 20% of 500 = _____
17. $66\frac{2}{3}$% of 120 = _____

18. 42% of 50 = _____
19. 50% of 1,800 = _____
20. 32% of 25 = _____

Problem Solving

21. A 20% down payment is required on the purchase of a new car. What is the amount of the down payment needed to buy a $21,000 car? _____

22. Jason has a 25% discount coupon for an amusement park ticket. How much will he save on a ticket that normally costs $32? _____

23. Marvin earned $800 one summer. He saved 75% of his earnings. How much money did Marvin save? _____

24. Eighty percent of the 300 students at Taft School ride the school bus. How many students is this? _____

25. Mabelle's food bill at a restaurant was $20. She decided to leave a 15% tip. How much tip did she leave? _____

 LITTLE SOMETHING DIFFERENT...

Use mental math to calculate the appropriate tip.

a. Choose an entrée, a dessert, and a beverage.

b. Find 20% of the total. This will be the tip.

c. Add the total and the tip. How much would your meal cost? _____

MENU	
Beverages	**Dessert**
Milk - $1.25	Cheesecake - $4.50
Cranberry Juice - $1.15	Apple Crisp - $3.00
	Pudding - $2.50
Entrées	
Spaghetti - $5.00	
Steak - $10.00	
Scampi - $9.25	

SKILL 15 PERCENTS GREATER THAN 100 OR LESS THAN 1

Mr. Lockwood's class at Kendall School is collecting aluminum cans to recycle. The goal is to collect 500 cans. So, 500 represents 100% of their goal.

Percents can be less than 1% or greater than 100%.

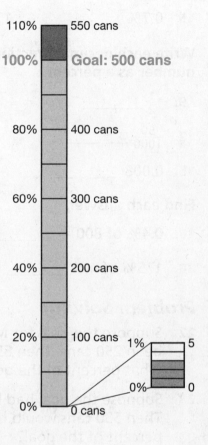

Example 1

On the first day, one student brought 3 cans.
Write 3 out of 500 as a percent.

$$\frac{3}{500} = \frac{3 \div 5}{500 \div 5} = \frac{0.6}{100} = 0.6\%$$

Read: *6 tenths percent.*

0.6% is less than 1% of the goal.

Example 2

By the end of the second week, the students had collected 550 cans. Write 550 as a percent of 500.

$$\frac{550}{500} = \frac{550 \div 5}{500 \div 5} = \frac{110}{100} = 110\%$$

Read: *one hundred ten percent*

Notice that 110% is more than 100% of the goal.

GUIDED PRACTICE

Write each fraction, mixed number, or whole number as a percent.

1. $\frac{2}{400} = \frac{2 \div 4}{400 \div 4} = \frac{0.5}{100} =$ _____

2. $2\frac{1}{2} = \frac{5}{2} = \frac{5 \times 50}{2 \times 50} = \frac{250}{100} =$ _____

3. $\frac{16}{500} = \frac{16 \div 5}{500 \div 5} = \frac{3.2}{100} =$ _____

4. $4 = \frac{4}{1} = \frac{4 \times 100}{1 \times 100} = \frac{400}{100} =$ _____

Write each decimal as a percent. (Hint: When you multiply by 100, move the decimal point two places to the right.)

5. 0.004 = _____

6. 2.09 = _____

7. 0.061 = _____

8. 3.57 = _____

Write each percent as a decimal.

9. 240% = 240 ÷ 100 = _____

10. 0.3% = 0.3 ÷ 100 = _____

Find each percent.

11. 0.9% of 120

0.009 × 120 = _____

12. 225% of 40

2.25 × 40 = _____

13. 0.2% of 134

_____ × _____ = _____

NOW YOU TRY IT!

Write each percent as a decimal.

1. 0.3% _____
2. 215% _____
3. 0.95% _____
4. 500% _____

5. 0.7% _____
6. 150% _____
7. 625% _____
8. 0.03% _____

Write each decimal, fraction, mixed number, or whole number as a percent.

9. $1\frac{1}{2}$ _____
10. $3\frac{1}{5}$ _____
11. $\frac{3}{200}$ _____

12. $\frac{50}{1000}$ _____
13. 1.82 _____
14. 5.6 _____

15. 0.008 _____
16. 0.0012 _____
17. 3 _____

Find each answer.

18. 0.4% of 800 = _____
19. 300% of 18 = _____

20. 175% of 4 = _____
21. 0.5% of 600 = _____

Problem Solving

22. Suppose the goal for Mr. Lockwood's class had been 250 cans. Then 550 cans would have been what percent of the goal? _____

23. Suppose the goal had been 1,000 cans. Then 550 cans would have been what percent of the goal? _____

24. Fran said that 150% of the 30 students in Mr. Lockwood's class participated in the can-collecting activity. Is this possible? Explain.

_____

25. Pinar said that 0.5% of the entire school brought in most of the cans. Is this possible? Explain.

_____

_____

TEST PREP

26. Find 180% of 300.

   A 5.4
   C 54
   B 54,000
   D 540

27. Find 18.3% of 18.

   F 1.01
   H 3.29
   G 1.80
   J 5

NAME _____   DATE _____

SECTION C WRAP-UP

TEST PREP

Circle each correct answer.

1. Write 0.237 as a percent.

   A 23.7   **C** 237

   B 2.37%   **D** 23.7%

2. Find 75% of 36.

   F 48   **H** 270

   G 27   **J** 108

3. Write 76% as a fraction in simplest form.

   A $\frac{76}{100}$ **C** $\frac{19}{25}$

   B $\frac{38}{50}$ **D** 17%

4. Find 62% of 47.

   F 2,914   **H** 29.14

   G 3.76   **J** 37.6

5. Seven wins out of 10 games is what percent?

   A 70%   **C** 30%

   B $\frac{7}{10}$ **D** 70

6. Write 325% as a decimal?

   F 3,250   **H** 325

   G 0.325   **J** 3.25

7. Find $33\frac{1}{3}$% of 60.

   A 10   **C** 30

   B 20   **D** 19.8

8. Find 200% of 50.

   F 50   **H** 1,000

   G 100   **J** 10,000

9. Find 15% of 0.4.

   A 0.6   **C** 0.06

   B 6   **D** 0.006

10. Write 53.5% as a decimal.

    F 0.535   **H** 5,350

    G 5.35   **J** 53.5

11. Which is the best estimate of 34% of 51?

    A 1,500   **C** 20

    B 10   **D** 17

12. What percent of the figure is shaded?

    F 20%   **H** 4 out of 5

    G $\frac{4}{5}$ **J** 80%

13. Find 0.3% of 100.

    A 0.003   **C** 300

    B 0.3   **D** 30

14. Which is the best estimate of 19.3% of 87?

    F 1.8   **H** 18

    G 12   **J** 1.6

SECTION C WRAP-UP

SOMETHING DIFFERENT...

PERCENT BARS!

Percent bars are a great way to solve percent problems, even really tough ones. All you really need is some paper for your sketches.

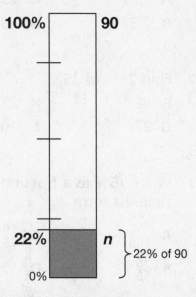

Suppose you want to find 22% of 90.

Step 1: Mark the percent bar with 0% and 100% at the bottom and the top.

Step 2: Find where 22% is. Don't worry, *estimate* it by locating 25%. 22% is between 0% and 25% and close to 25%. Right? Good enough! Make a mark. Also, color in the percent of the bar you are to find.

Step 3: On the other side of the percent bar find 90. You don't know where it is? It's the same as the whole bar. So mark it at the top with the 100%.

Step 4: Now write a proportion right from the percent bar. Use *n* for the number you do not know.

Put the percent numbers on the left side of the bar in the left ratio.

Put the numbers from the right side of the percent bar into the right ratio.

$$\frac{100}{22} = \frac{90}{n}$$

$$100n = 22 \times 90$$

$$n = \frac{22 \times 90}{100}$$

$$n = 19.8$$

Now try some of your own. Use the bars below.

1. 41% of 65   **2.** 35% of 80   **3.** 72% of 150   **4.** 11% of 67

  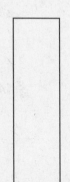 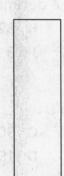